## Carol Edwards

Carol is the creator of Feminine Riles, on Instagram. It has over 5,000 followers. Her cartoons use gorgeous graphics and mind-bending content to go behind the accepted narrative of "being female". Above all, her work illuminates the key issues facing half of humanity, while raising readers' eyebrows and skewering convention. Each cartoon, though seemingly small, tells a broader story: Readers say they not only challenge and enlighten, they start conversations.

Carol is also a multiple award-winning professor of finance, with over 25 years of teaching experience. Students and colleagues have praised her materials for their creative approach to delivering complex, difficult concepts in a way which is interesting, concise, accessible, and "awesome!"

Carol recently retired from the graduate program at the globally top-ranked Beedie School. That puts her in a small coterie of women instructing students in advanced finance. Moreover, in the 1980s, she was one of a very few females in the world to work in the testosterone-charged field of portfolio management.

A life-long feminist, Carol has considerable experience with the issues she cartoons about.

## Nicole Mallinson

Nicole is a graphic designer from Vancouver, BC. She is 30 years old and running her own content creation company while being a mom. When she's not creating, she loves hockey, snowboarding, travelling and all kinds of adrenaline adventures.

Nicole joined the *Feminine Riles* team back in 2020 as the graphic artist and has continued on to help as a social media manager.

She loves being part of the fight to empower women and ask the tough questions on why our society works the way it does.

# FEMININE RILES
cartoons to promote thought

## Carol Edwards
### Nicole Mallinson

dixi books

*The Voice of the New Age*

**Feminine Riles**
Content by Carol Edwards
Illustrations by Carol Edwards and Nicole Mallinson

Copyright © 2022 Dixi Books
All rights reserved. No part of this book may be reproduced or transmitted to any form or by any means, electronic or mechanical, including photocopying, recording, or by any information and retrieval system, without written permission from the publisher.
First published in January 2023
ISBN: 978-1-913680-50-3

**Dixi Books**
293 Green Lanes, Palmers Green
London, England, N13 4XS
www.dixibooks.com
info@dixibooks.com

## DEDICATION

Dedicated to the memory of my parents, Sheila and David, who taught me to think for myself.

And in loving gratitude to everyone – every race, creed, colour, sex, sexual orientation, gender – who has fought for our rights, for equality, justice and fairness. Thank you for your service – often at great risk to yourself, including imprisonment, torture and death. May I be worthy to follow in your footsteps.

*~ Carol Edwards*


Dedicated to my baby girl, Pandora, who was born during the creation of this book. She gave me an undying respect for the female body and the amazing gift of life that we as women are able to bring into this world. We need books like this to challenge the patriarchy and create a better world for her and all the women of tomorrow to grow up in.

*~ Nicole Mallinson*

# INTRODUCTION

Patriarchy [*pay*-tree-r-key, noun]: A word, like *war, rape, lynch* or *genocide*, which encompasses within a few letters so much evil, so much stupidity, so much destruction, pain and hurt.

Patriarchy is a *dysfunctional* social system which originated a brief 3 to 5 millennia ago. It is *a human artefact* built on the concepts of male superiority and misogyny; militarism, slavery, the dominance of a few, the expendability of the many; the objectification of "the other", including our *Mother the Earth*; and the hatred of anyone not of our tribe, as well as those of the tribe who do not slavishly and mindlessly follow its rules for behaviour.

In Nature, working with *Gaia* to preserve the environment for your descendants, cooperation between and within species to maximize group success, and survival of the fittest individuals are the critical mantras when it comes to producing future generations. On the individual side, an inflexible rule for a male is that a strong, healthy, intelligent, competent and capable female is *the* way to ensure that his offspring are both vigorous and have a maximum chance of surviving to reproduce.

Our species has been around for over 500 millennia. In a mere 4 of those millennia, less than 1% of human existence, the patriarchy has created the perfect recipe for extinction by turning the natural order upside down, weakening our gene pool by:

- Killing-off the strongest males in war, leaving the elderly, decrepit and weak to reproduce, while finding "sexiness" in females who are physically unfit – weak, fragile, sickly, frail – and mentally incapable – spineless, incompetent, helpless, witless.

- Poisoning our children's food with additives, preservatives, colouring, salt, sugar, etc., while taking that food from an environment made increasingly toxic by artificial fertilizers, pesticides and pollution.

- Siring sub-systems, such as mercantilism, colonialism, and capitalism, and whatever you want to call what operates in places like China and Russia, *all of which, regardless of how they self-describe*, destroy the future for our descendants so as to line the pockets of a few dominant males.

- Treating *Gaia* like an object, something to be manipulated, exploited, used and abused, destroying our world – its land, water, air and biosphere – the world our children will have to grow up in and then try to raise their children in.

Our mission is to confront the ills created by patriarchy – to make this world a better place by creating cartoons to promote thought.

Understand we all swim in a toxic pool of patriarchal sludge – attitudes, beliefs, prejudices. We want our cartoons to encourage you to think deeply and critically about what you read, hear and see. We want you to look at what we have so long taken for granted. We want you to get riled-up at the astonishing silliness and senselessness of the things the patriarchy has taught us to accept.

And that is especially true with respect to its daughters: The absurdity, the cruelty, the inexplicability of how we think about half the human race, behave towards females, organize women's lives and choose to shape our societies on a truly strange platform of outdated and sexist ideas.

*~ Feminineriles.com*

The patriarchy is a hierarchical system in which a small, dominant male group (**MASTERS**) holds power, while all others (**UNDERLINGS**) are excluded, inferiorized and expected to work for the masters as cheaply as possible, preferably for free.

**MASTERS** are raised to be "superior", privileged, the ideal template crafted by God.

They are taught to feel entitled to satisfy their every desire, *regardless of the damage* it inflicts on minds, bodies or souls – including their own. They are trained to suppress all emotions except anger and hate; to be violent and warlike; to exploit, use and abuse the "weak", including other males in their group.

Masters are wired to bully, control, hurt, betray and expect sexual conquest along with emotional detachment. They are not wired for mutual, respectful or healthy intimacy with anyone, including their own cohort.

*Their wiring is toxic – unnatural and pathological, turning them into narcissistic and selfish egomaniacs committed to perpetuating the system which favours them.*

*/continued ...*

**UNDERLINGS** consist of women, BIPOC and minorities. They are seen as "substandard" beings, the Creator's afterthought, or a curse sent by the Gods.

They are taught to kowtow to the masters in their every desire, *regardless of the damage* it inflicts on their minds, bodies or souls. They are trained to be subordinate – docile, submissive, fawning, smiling, non-questioning and obedient.

Underlings are wired to be good servants ruled by the masters, caring for their every need, including raising their offspring within the existing system.

They are not wired for strength, independent thought or action, or healthy intimacy with anyone, including their own cohort.

*Their wiring is toxic – unnatural and pathological, turning them into selfless and humble doormats devoted to perpetuating the system for their masters.*

The patriarchy behaves like an alien invader, turning us into creatures which willingly work against our own interests to assist it to propagate and spread.

Welcome to the horror show: ***Invasion of the Body Snatchers*** is real!

***NOTES: Invasion of the Body Snatchers*** *is a 1950's science fiction horror film in which an invasion of Earth is effected by aliens that "manufacture" copies of living people. The duplicate then replaces that person, having their physical characteristics and memories, but being a zombie which is devoid of all humanity. The film is ranked in the top 25 horror films. It is described as "still very scary", incorporating the concepts of dehumanization, brainwashing and the loss of personal autonomy and individual identity.*

*Hmmmmm, now doesn't that sound just like the patriarchy?*

Film Poster: Distributed by Allied Artists Pictures Corporation/Scan via Heritage Auctions. Public Domain: https://commons.wikimedia.org/w/index.php?curid=86642192

Patriarchy is a cultural invention. It is not natural, inevitable, God-given or based on biological differences between men and women.

It is a social construct, **man-made** between 3 and 5 millennia ago, when tribes of warlike and brutal males invaded, subjugated and destroyed the settled, more civilized and egalitarian societies which existed before.

As professional killers, whose closest ties were with their brothers-in-arms, they scorned all things "womanly" – they were misogynists.

They created in their own image a dominant (have no gods before me), brutal, blood-thirsty, violent, vengeful, misogynistic, male god who decreed contempt for females, anyone not of the tribe, and anyone of the tribe who did not conform to "HIS" rules.

Their male priesthood very conveniently revealed that the men of the tribe, and their male descendants, were the masters of the universe, divinely appointed (chosen) to subdue, oppress, enslave and slaughter the peoples around them, to dispossess the Mother Goddess, whom the conquered had worshipped, and to dominate the Earth, along with all within it.

*/continued ...*

Our culture is rooted in an *ancient evil*: A self-serving scheme by ruthless, killer-conquerors who purposely designed a world of inequality. One built on ensuring their enrichment and empowerment, combined with an institutionalized system of oppression, enslavement, loathing and even extinction for everyone else.

> "As a [way to organize society], patriarchy is as outdated as feudalism ... a 4,000-year-old system of ideas that won't just go away."
> ~ *Dr. Gerda Lerner (pioneering historian, feminist and expert in patriarchy)*

No – this evil, brutal and antiquated social system won't "just go away".

It is past time to take action to turn this horror show off.

> ***Attention everyone – time to stand-up and leave the theatre!***

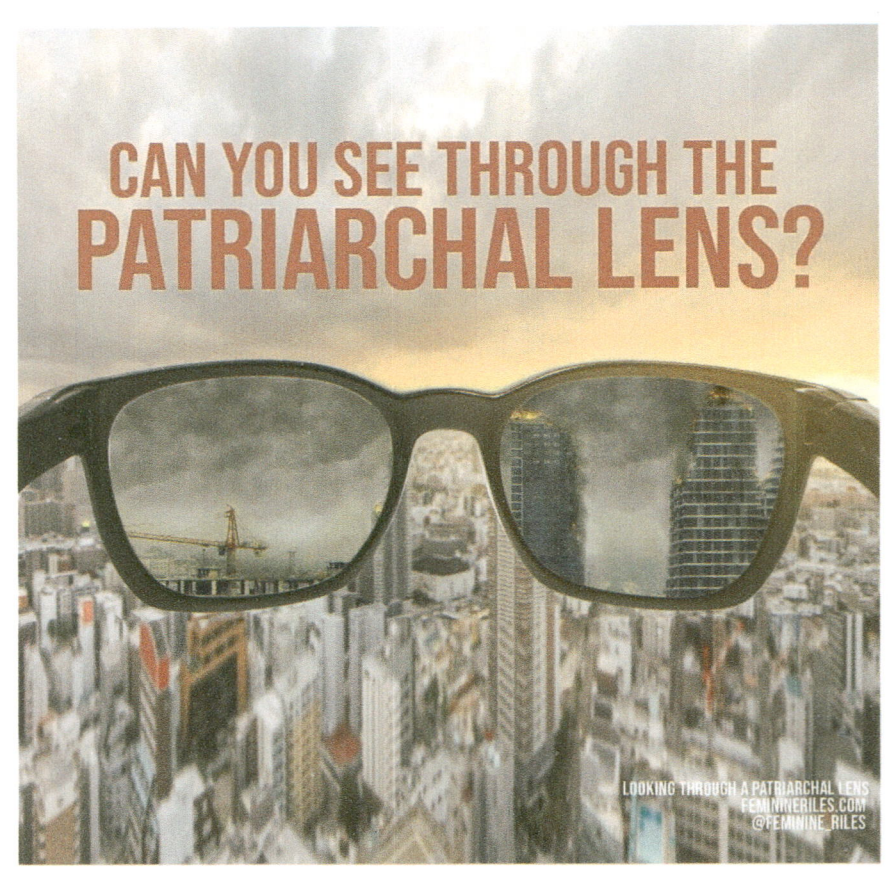

Patriarchy is a social system created by brutal conquerors using three concepts:

**1. Slavery**
In a *slave society*, those defined as superior by their class/religion/wealth/education/genetic heritage (e.g., male *and* Aryan, Caucasian or European) are masters – privileged, entitled, despots. Everyone else is an underling who may be used, abused and disposed of at the whim of a master.

Underlings are always seen as potentially dangerous – liable to rise up and kill the masters. They are rigidly controlled, indoctrinated into believing in their inferiority, and drilled to be servile, obedient and non-questioning.

Paranoia about rebellion means all underlings are a threat. Masters and their authorized servants (police, military, courts) feel free to attack an underling, even one exhibiting the most innocent of behaviours. Any conduct outside accepted norms for a subordinate will be viciously and violently dealt with.

**2. Militarism**
A *militaristic society* is organized into layered ranks of masters and underlings: The King is supreme. His nobles control all below them, their knights control those below them … and so on for every level of society and every group in it.

The world is a bureaucratic triangle, with a few in the top levels giving orders and hoarding the wealth. A small layer of sycophants supports the top, while the multitude at the bottom are expected to do as they are told, uphold the system, toil to create the wealth, and feel gratitude for any crumbs which fall from above.

*/continued …*

### 3. Male dominance and misogyny

In a society of *male dominance* men are on top. *Misogyny* means that "femaleness" is treated with contempt – suppressed, enslaved, punished, silenced, kept ignorant and preferably locked-up and away from the public eye. A female in public, unaccompanied by her owner, may be harassed, raped, tortured, maimed or killed at the whim of any passing male. And she deserves it.

Patriarchy ties together a host of what before seemed to be isolated and dissimilar concepts, events and people.

Consider the following:

- Capitalism, communism, imperialism, colonialism, fascism, Nazism, totalitarianism, authoritarianism, bureaucracies.

- War, genocide, eugenics, racism, discrimination, rape culture, wife abuse, public sexual harassment, work harassment.

- The Klan, the Aryan Brotherhood, Daesh, the Taliban.

- Royalty, class society, billionaires, social inequality and poverty.

- George Floyd, Breonna Taylor, Ahmaud Arbery, Harvey Weinstein, Jeffrey Epstein, Roger Ailes, Trump, the Koch brothers.

Do you see the pattern?

*/continued ...*

Stare through a patriarchal lens at history, at how our societies function, at every news story, every political event, every economic one, how you and others like you are treated ... Are the pieces of the puzzle starting to fall into place?

***Doesn't the world suddenly start to make perfect sense once you understand how patriarchy functions?***

A male ruler may be demented, syphilitic, paranoid, blood thirsty, perverted, stupid, mentally ill.

He may destroy his country's economy, gut its currency, stifle rights and freedoms, disappear his opponents. He may arbitrarily imprison, torture, maim and kill those around him, invade his neighbours and slaughter countless young men in pointless wars.

The patriarchy insists on this:

One dreads to think how much worse it would have been had a woman been in power.


**NOTES:** *Naturally, a woman would be worse. (So saith the patriarchy.)*

A patriarchal society relentlessly fetishizes chastity, virginity and fidelity.

Men mouth their loyalty to these virtues.

Women are expected to live them.

***NOTES:*** *Women – do as we say, not as we do. (So saith the patriarchy.)*

**PATRIARCHY**

A social system in which:

Females, no matter how intelligent, attractive or desirable, are brainwashed into seeing themselves as dumpy, dumb and undesirable, in need of a new haircut, different make-up, a more effective diet, a better perfume, a new outfit or even surgery.

Males, no matter how unintelligent, unattractive or undesirable, are empowered to see themselves as captivating, clever and charming, in need of nothing.

To ask for advice is to show weakness.

To listen to others is to show weakness.

To care for others is to show weakness.

To be gentle, compassionate and kind is to show weakness.

To express any emotion other than cold stoicism, anger, hostility or hatred is to show weakness.

How indescribably sad the patriarchy has made it to be a man.

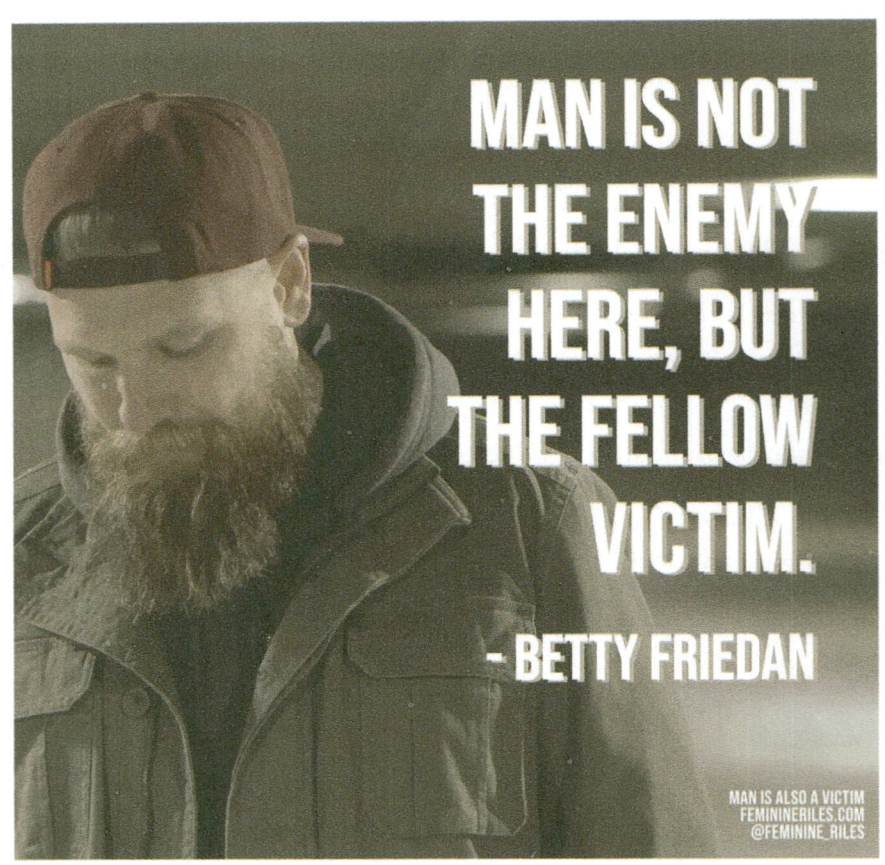

The world men inhabit is rather bleak. It is a world full of doubt and confusion, where vulnerability must be hidden, not shared; where competition, not co-operation, is the order of the day; where men sacrifice the possibility of knowing their own children and sharing in their upbringing, for the sake of a job they may have chosen by chance, which may not suit them and which in many cases dominates their lives to the exclusion of much else.
~ *Anna Ford*

The things I particularly like about men are their differentness, their simplicity, their cleverness, their ability to amuse and re-tell life better than it is, their sense of fun, their intelligence, their dependence on women, their boyishness – even childishness – their ability to devote themselves single-mindedly to their interests, their charm, their insecurity, their character and, above all, when they reveal it, their gentleness and vulnerability.
~ *Anna Ford*

Man is not the enemy here, but the fellow victim.
~ *Betty Friedan*


**NOTES:** *This is **not** a battle **against** men. It's a battle **for** equality.*

*Women don't want **more** than men ... they just want **as much as** them.*

*And what we're fighting for will help them too! Particularly those who feel pressured by toxic masculine stereotypes ... or who simply want to participate in a healthy society and economy.*

Men should be flocking to feminism ...

Male dominated societies report the LOWEST levels of male sexual satisfaction.

These societies revile pleasure as SINFUL.

They separate male from female, keeping them ignorant of sex and of how to pleasure each other.

Studies show that sexual satisfaction for men is HIGHEST in those societies where feminist values are strongest, in those which value gender equality the most.

Men experience the GREATEST sexual fulfillment in the bedroom when women experience the GREATEST fulfillment outside of it.

Until the lion has a historian of its own, tales of the hunt will always glorify the hunter.
~ *African proverb*

The very ink with which all history is written is merely fluid prejudice.
~ *Mark Twain*

History does not repeat itself. Historians repeat each other.
~ *Arthur Balfour*

The victor will never be asked if he told the truth.
~ *Hitler*

God cannot change the past, but historians can.
~ *Samuel Butler*

**History**: The art of recording things which were not so in the service of those in power.

**Just-Not-So Stories.**


**NOTES:** *What men who made history say about "history" - and it ain't what you've been brainwashed to think it is!*

*History **isn't** unbiased, it **isn't** "just the facts", and it **isn't** comprehensive, accurate or even the truth. Recorded history is someone's opinion about what happened based on the data they can access, what they choose to use of that data and how they decide to report that information.*

*Women make history; they do not make his-story*

The patriarchy has long tried to deny Woman a place in what Man calls "history".

For millennia, she was told she was confined to the house, deprived of an education and the right to work; forbidden to participate in government, the economy, the military, the arts, the sciences, philosophy or academia; not allowed to publish work under her own name or to patent what she created.

Any woman who bridled at these restrictions met with huge familial and social resistance. She could expect to be ostracised, threatened, imprisoned, beaten or killed into her accepted place.

*Oh yes, the patriarchy tried hard to prevent women from making history.*

And when so many of them did, against overwhelming odds, their amazing contributions were reviled, deemed irrelevant, glossed-over, ignored, buried, minimized, confined to a footnote, denied, erased or attributed to a man.

Of course, women made *history* – read the hundreds of thousands of their amazing stories on *Wikipedia*!

What they didn't make is ***his-story.***

---

**NOTES:** *Far more people - women, minorities, slaves - have contributed to history than those few whose privileged status gained them entrée to his-story. Like the lion, we need an historian of our own.*

History is written by the winners.

Women have long been legislated, regulated and mandated into the loser's position.

One should not ask why few women made it into "his-story".

One should wonder how any made it at all.

**Man 1:** I tied him up and then punched him senseless. It was easy to beat him.

**Man 2:** Well, duh ... no big accomplishment, you had the advantage!

**Man 1:** My horse lost the race. It was handicapped with too much weight.

**Man 2:** Well, duh ... no surprise there, it had a disadvantage!

**Man 1:** In our family, girls were deprived of education and every opportunity, except to be a wife and mother. The family's resources were for the boys. And, you know what, none of the women in our family ever accomplished as much as the men did.

**Man 2:** Well, duh ... that's women for you – just can't compete with us guys!

*NOTES: Men understand the concepts of advantage and disadvantage, of handicap and windfall, of level playing field and inequality, of fair play and injustice ... except when it comes to how they treat women.*

## Competition?

Men love to applaud and praise it. But the threat of *real* competition scares them. So, historically, men eliminated at least one-half of the human race from the race.

Man's dirty little secret when it comes to competition resembles their economic attitudes: Talk about free trade while instituting subsidies, tariffs and quotas.

## Subsidies:

- In trade, advantage a product by providing it with financial assistance not provided to others.
- In patriarchy, boys get the lion's share of a society's resources; girls get left out.

## Tariffs:

- In trade, disadvantage a product with a higher cost structure.
- In patriarchy, girls get lumbered with the housework before they can do paid work.

## Quotas:

- In trade, restrict product entry.
- In patriarchy, institute a policy of no girls allowed.

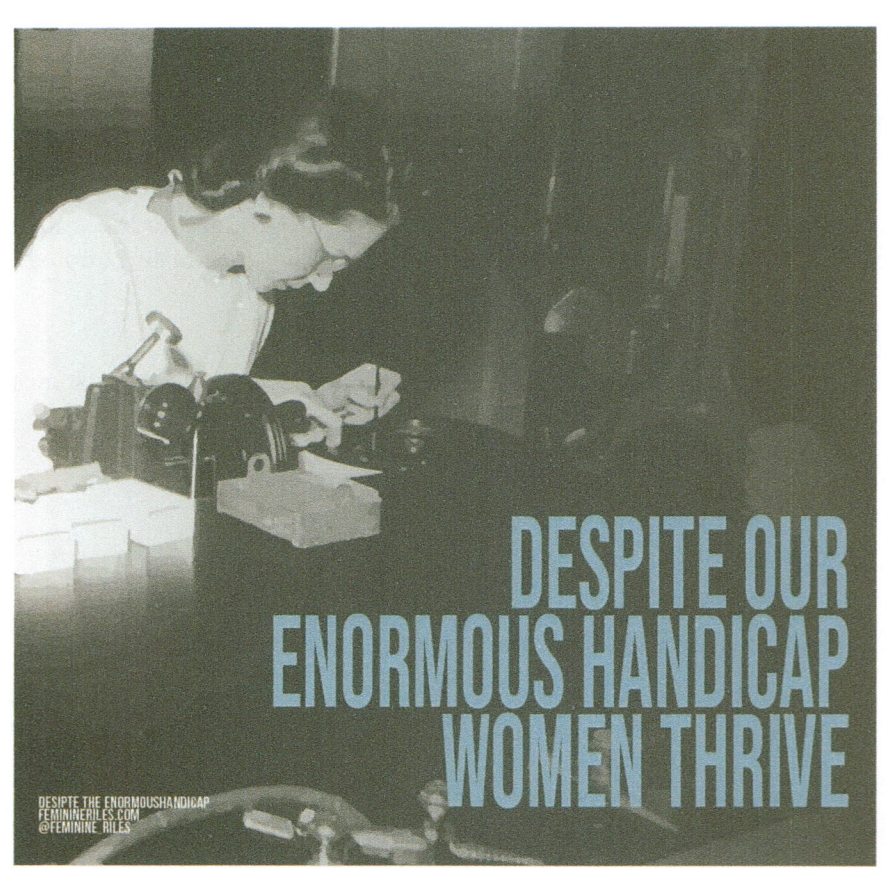

Men ask women, "Where *are* all your great entrepreneurs, writers, musicians, doctors, philosophers, scientists, artists?"

This is akin to a plantation-owner in the Deep South demanding of his slaves, "So, where *are* all your great entrepreneurs, writers, musicians, doctors, philosophers, scientists, artists?"

The amazing thing is that, despite the enormous handicaps imposed on them by Society, women and other minorities have created so many great entrepreneurs, writers, musicians, doctors, philosophers, scientists and artists.

***NOTES**: Just imagine how different this world would be if we'd have been given an equal opportunity to contribute to its future …*

# WHAT IF THE TABLES WERE REVERSED?

Imagine if the tables had been reversed, if for millennia boys had been told from birth:

- How useless, unwanted and inferior they were.
- That they were restricted to the house.
- That their only legitimate future was marriage, childcare and house work.
- That fewer resources would be devoted to them than to their sisters.
- That they were not entitled to an education, a trade or a job.
- That they could not do art, music, writing, philosophy, science or research.
- That they were not allowed to publish or patent their work.

Privileged women could then hypocritically berate their disadvantaged brothers by taunting, "Where *are* your famous men? Where *are* all your great scientists, inventors, entrepreneurs, philosophers, writers, composers and artists?"

We will never know all that women did accomplish.

For millennia, a woman could not claim credit for what she did – for her inventions, her art, her writing, her work. She was forced to use a male pseudonym or let a male – husband, brother, father, son, friend – claim the credit.

Or, famously so, *Anonymous* was a woman.

Even worse, we will never know what women didn't accomplish because they were prohibited from trying or were too afraid or too repressed to try.

Weep, my Sisters, weep for the loss of your history, for the legacy stolen from you by your Brothers.

**NOTES**: *Think of what the world has lost ... think of what all those women, minorities and slaves might have accomplished had they been given a fair shot at education, opportunity and options ... the books not written, the cures not found, the inventions not created, the avenues not explored.*

*Is it right that those who stole this chance should then use their bully pulpit to decry the "inferior" or "negligible" accomplishments of their victims?*

Under the patriarchy, Men have stolen from their Sisters the legacies of history, of discovery, of authorship, of creation and of invention.

They impoverished us; their actions left us lesser mortals, constrained to a tiny world limited to the walls of our household.

And then they derided us for our poverty of experience and called us inferior.

Women – read about them in their hundreds of thousands on *Wikipedia* – and all but a few of them excluded from his-story.

But, did you know that men have also written women out of economics?

"Woman's work" does *not* get counted in the measurement of GDP.

That's right, ladies – the thousands of hours you devote every year *to ensuring the success of the fundamental unit of the economy, the family,* counts for \*\***NOTHING**\*\* in the National Accounts.

Why?

Because, silly you, you didn't get paid for doing it – and unpaid work, no matter how important to Society, is deemed valueless, not worthy of being included in calculating GDP, the economic activity of a country!

All hail male logic: If we don't pay you for it, if instead, we steal it from you, well, then it ain't real, and we don't have to record it – nyah nyah nyah nyah nyah!

Imagine a housewife who diligently cares for her house and children.

She makes **_no_** contribution to the economy according to GDP, the traditional measure of economic wealth.

Now imagine she drowns the children and burns the house down.

*This would lead to an increase in economic wealth!*

The cost of firefighters and vehicles, the investigation, the clean-up and rebuilding of the house, the lawyers, the court case … all would contribute to GDP.

Keeping her locked-up, fed and clothed; providing psychiatric treatment, social-workers, building maintenance, prison guards, security, etc. … all would contribute to GDP.

But, would anyone other than an economist or an idiot think that her actions brought anything but harm to her family, her community and the economy?

**NOTES**: *The way the patriarchy has chosen to measure economic activity is inherently sexist and anti-environment: Two key factors which are excluded from GDP are unpaid work and environmental indicators.*

*/continued …*

*Women do the majority of this unpaid work, which is **conservatively** estimated to represent between 20% and 50% of conventionally calculated GDP. If our work were **not** invisible, GDP would look significantly different from what is currently reported.*

*It should be realized that it didn't have to be this way – when GDP was being devised, an eminent female researcher, Phyllis Deane (a brilliant economist excluded from his-story and the Nobel prize, of course!), maintained that it was an error to ignore unpaid work, that it was illogical to do so, and that if governments wanted to design policies to increase economic welfare, and to ensure an equitable distribution of resources, the work of ALL who contributed to the success of an economy had to be counted. But no attention was paid to her insights.*

*More recently, other female scholars, such as Silvia Federici, have argued that the measured production of men **is actually impossible** without women's work – that is, without a wife to care for the children and the home, how would any man have the time or the energy to hold a full-time job? One of the best-known criticisms of GDP is to be found in Marilyn Waring's 1988 book, **If Women Counted**. Another significant work on the harms created when women are ignored in data analysis is **Invisible Women: Data Bias in a World Designed for Men** by Caroline Criado Perez, which shows that "bias and discrimination are baked into our systems. And women pay the price, in time and money and often with their lives."*

*Because woman are invisible, because our work is not measured, or valued, this has distorted our perception of the economy, leading to poor policy, weak family arrangements, false indicators of how well-off we are, and reduced human welfare.*

*Furthermore, the way GDP is calculated, especially its exclusion of environmental factors, means that it does not measure actual human well-being – it tells us nothing about whether we and our children are safe, healthy, educated and well-cared for, or whether our natural world is being destroyed to line a few pockets.*

*It is well past time that this idiocy should be corrected.*

> *(a) Holding a full-time job is demanding, hard-work.*
> *(b) Caring for house, hubby and heirs is demanding, hard work and a full-time job.*

Studies show:

Men do (a) and contribute little *to* (b). Women do (a) and the majority *of* (b).

Men have been privileged to focus on (a) because they can rely on some woman to step in and do (b) for them.

Women still have to do both and cannot rely on anyone to step in and do (b) for them.

- Cultural Advantage: Men
- Cultural Handicap: Women

Men have no more right to crow to women about their "success" in the business world, and how that success is derived from their superior "attachment" to their work, than a fighter who has beaten an opponent with his hands tied behind his back.

**NOTES**: *The Double Burden of Career and Housework*

*We all know there are no days off in parenting—and research shows just how hard moms are working.*

*/continued …*

*A study released by Welch's looked at 2,000 American moms of kids between 5 and 12 years old, and found the **average hours moms work per week is 98.** As in the equivalent of two-and-a-half full-time jobs.*

*~ Mother.ly (https://www.mother.ly/state-of-motherhood/surveys-tallies-the-hours-moms-work-per-weekand-its-probably-a-shock-to-anyone-but-us/)*

*A double burden (AKA double day, second shift or double duty) is the workload many women face working to earn money while also shouldering an outsized share of responsibility for childcare and domestic labor.*

*For those who would like to read the seminal work in this field of study, check out the updated version of the book **The Second Shift: Working Families and the Revolution at Home** by sociologist and University of California, Berkeley, professor Arlie Hochschild. It cites a range of recent studies and statistics and includes a new afterword in which the author assesses how much – and how little – has changed for women today.*

> ***Every woman's dream is that a man will take her in his arms,***
> ***throw her into bed, and clean the house while she sleeps.***
> *~ Meme on the Internet*

Men have wives at home to do the housework, to prepare the food and care for the children. This allows them to climb the ladder of success unencumbered.

A woman, unless she chooses to be childless, or is wealthy, climbs that same ladder with a huge burden on her back.

Isn't it time for men to come out of the cosset?

Guys! Introducing the *Traditional Wife©*, the marvellous, high quality, patented accessory!

It cooks! It cleans! It will change how you do housework forever!

So fast! So easy! You'll just love your *Wife©*!

But wait! There is more!

It polishes the ego! It maintains your lifestyle, perfect every-time! And with this one time offer, you also get great sexual entertainment!

But that is not all!

Imagine, with a *Wife©*, you can even bear and raise offspring, without the drudgery, thus freeing you to find success and to get that promotion!

You'll be amazed!

Order one today ... you'll be so glad you did!

**Wife:**
A critical evolutionary development which allowed the male of the species to successfully avoid the question:

*"How do you do it – combine a family with a career?"*

Unfortunately, this valuable adaptation has mutated and seems to have developed a mind of its own.

*NOTES: The Wife - A Valuable Adaptation for Work/Life Balance.*

### *Behind every great man, there is a great woman.*
*~ Anonymous*

*While the origin is unknown, the first printed citation of "Behind every great man, there's a great woman," is from a Texas newspaper quoting Meryll Frost, a Canadian-born football player, who uttered these words after he was awarded the 'Most Courageous Athlete of the Year' in 1946: "While I'm not a great man, there's a great woman behind me."*

*This shows that over 75 years ago, there were people who realized how critical the role of a wife was to a man's ability to succeed.*

*By the 1960s and 1970s the women's movement adopted the slogan: "Behind every great man is an even greater woman."*

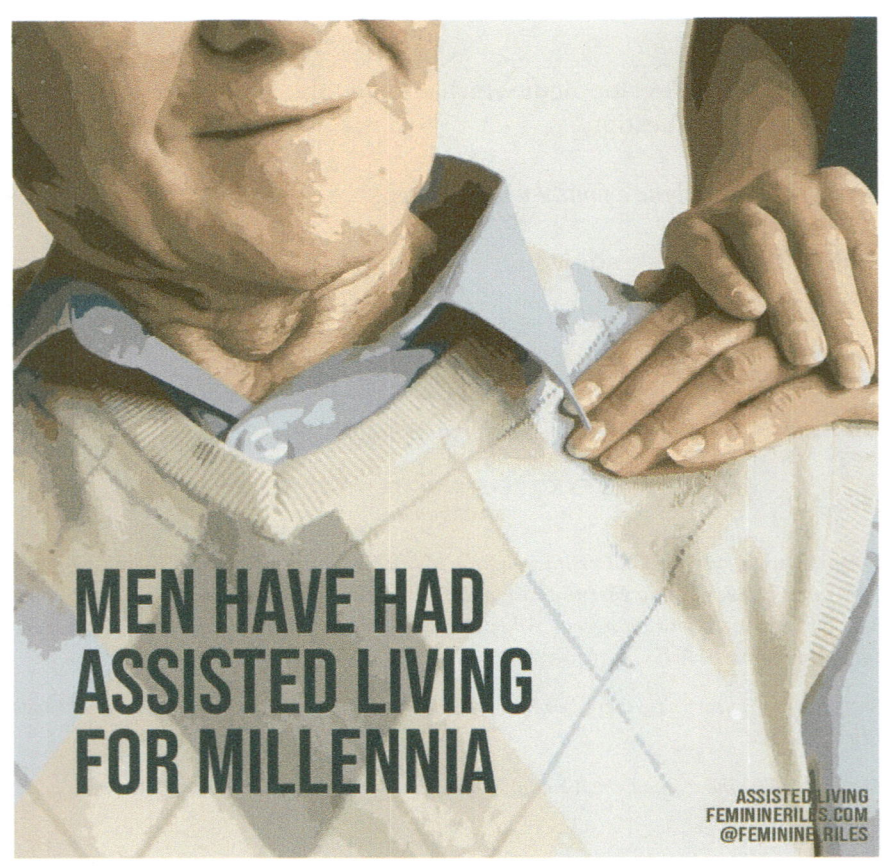

**ASSISTED LIVING:** Provides ongoing help with daily living for those who wish to retain their independence.

Typical services include:

- Cooking, housekeeping and laundry  • Personal care, dressing and grooming
- Minor medical care  • Health and exercise programs   • Transportation
- Educational, social and cultural activities.

Considered appropriate for anyone who no longer wishes to live on their own, but who does not need medical care.

More economical than hiring a housekeeper, a chauffeur, a personal assistant and a nurse.

Men have had assisted living for millennia.

It's called marriage.

> *"Women know what men have long forgotten. The ultimate economic and spiritual unit of any civilization is still the family."*
> ~ Clare Boothe Luce

An economy's future and its quality of life largely rest on the unpaid labour of women. Yet our huge contribution registers *nowhere* in GDP.

It is 'woman's work' to birth the next generation, to fashion a haven – a safe, clean, warm and loving environment – in which a family can blossom.

It is 'woman's work' to ensure that children are cared for, loved and grow up to be healthy, law-abiding and productive.

It is 'woman's work' to create the meals which produce strong bodies and minds.

Without our role, productivity would decline and social costs would rise.

Our contribution may be unmeasured, unrecorded and unpaid, yet it is absolutely and undeniably crucial to the functioning of a healthy, successful Society.

Indeed, 'woman's work' is far more essential to our species' survival, to our happiness and to our quality of life, than work performed in a mine, a factory, an office or a store.

**Why are we invisible?**

Never forget: People take their behavioural cues from economic signals.

Send out the wrong signals and you will get the wrong response.

Neglect of household production severely distorts our measures of both economic wealth and social well-being.

The family is the foundation of a Society. In its success can be found the success of that Society.

If we want to strengthen the Society, then some way must be found to measure Woman's unpaid contribution to it.

Some way must be found to make us visible, to give our contribution credibility, to give it respect, to give it value.

That is the ONLY WAY proper laws, policies and family-friendly arrangements can develop.


***NOTES***: *History vs. His-story. And now, Economics vs. He-conomics.*

*Critical underlying concept:*

> ***Male defined women = mal-defined women.***

'Woman's work' *is* work and it is worth a lot to our Society: If women were to disappear and men had to do the housework, as well as birth and raise the kids, what would happen to GDP as currently measured?

It would fall significantly as men had to withdraw from the paid economy to perform the unpaid and unrecognized wifely duties.

But you can bet if men were doing the bulk of the housework and child-care that they'd soon find some way to measure it – and it would become damned well-paid work to boot!

*NOTES*: *Safe bet - if men did it, they'd **measure it and pay it properly.***

# JUDGE DECLARES BEING A HOUSEWIFE IS A FULL-TIME JOB WORTHY OF COMPENSATION

24 September 2021

Teresia Matheka, a Kenyan High Court Judge, recently declared that being a housewife, caring for a home, husband and children, must be considered work as those tasks would otherwise be outsourced, meaning families would have to pay someone to do them.

Thus, being a wife is full-time employment and she should be paid a salary every month.

Judge Matheka said it is unreasonable to deny the important contribution a wife provides to the financial success of a household. She further stated it would be unfair to consider only monetary inputs as valuable - that one has to contribute money to a marriage to find value.

In addition, she urged other judges to consider pregnancy as equivalent to working, given that surrogates are hired and paid to bear children.

According to the Judge, housewives *should not be saying* they don't work because they do not bring money into the home. They provide critical services which need to be recognized as valuable economic activity.

Her ruling was in response to a husband who claimed all of the family property in a divorce. He said it was purchased entirely with his earnings, while his wife contributed nothing: She was not employed because she stayed at home and took care of the children and family.

*/continued ...*

Justice Matheka ruled the property be sold, and the money shared equally, or that one spouse should buy out the other by paying half the value to that other.

Why is this important?

Because Kenya is part of the British Commonwealth. Thus, its judicial rulings have relevance to cases heard in other courts in the Commonwealth, meaning most of the World.

*NOTES: Being a housewife **is** a full-time job worthy of compensation.*

*For all the idiots tempted to post the moronic questions, "Who will pay for it? And how?", let's provide an answer and save them some typing: The same question was asked by The South about its slaves ... and, you know, the problem got sorted out ...*

*From slaves to serfs, the issue of who pays once a group of people goes from unpaid to paid labour **has always** been resolved ... it's called human ingenuity ... so have faith, this question will get resolved as well ... and if you google it, you will find that lots of great ideas have been proposed for how to compensate those (both male and female) who devote themselves to caring for family.*

*That having been said, this is amazing news on the legal front as the law recognizes that what a housewife does **is** work, deserving of both recognition and compensation. America, the rest of the world, and economics, it's your move – the precedent is now there ... when do you follow suit?*

*Every mother is a working mother!*

Source: https://www.news24.com/parent/family/relationships/kenyan-judge-declares-that-being-a-housewife-is-a-payable-full-time-job-20210930

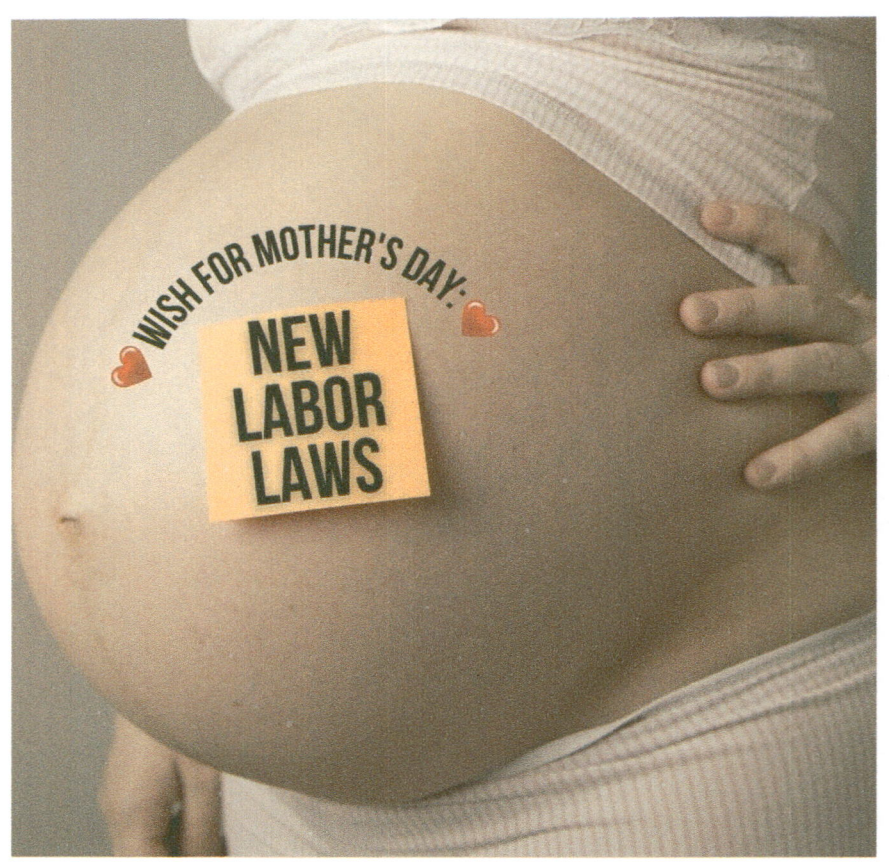

Before the 20th century, it is estimated between 1,000 and 2,000 women per 100,000 died due to pregnancy.

Childbirth was the leading cause of death for females aged 15 to 45 for most of human history, killing between 1 in 3 and 1 in 8.

It was so dangerous - *more risky than combat* - that a woman would make out her will as soon as she knew she was pregnant.

Bearing a child is still one of the most dangerous things a human being can do.

Approximately every 1.5 minutes, a woman dies due to pregnancy: 830 women/day. For every woman who dies, 20 to 30 suffer complications with serious or long-lasting consequences: 16 to 25 thousand women/day. (The above stats may be 30% - 50% too low due to reporting issues.)

*Sacrifice*: Giving-up something you value highly, *often your life*, usually for the sake of your people or a cause.

We accord young men *who risk the ultimate sacrifice*, who choose to become soldiers, who put their lives on the line for the future of their country, with recognition, pay and benefits.

Time for new labor laws?

Time to accord young women *who risk the ultimate sacrifice*, who choose to become mothers, who put their lives on the line for the future of their country, with the same appreciation?

Before the invention of WMD, more women died in childbirth in our species' history than men died on the battlefield.

So many untold numbers of our fore-mothers laid down their lives to ensure the future of their tribe, their society, their country - yet, who is it who gets remembered and honoured?

The ones who died giving death, not those who died in similar agony, but giving life.

Where are our statues to *The Unknown Mother*?

**NOTES**: *Females have always been front-line warriors in the survival of humanity - laying down their lives, souls and dreams to give birth, to raise the young and to care for the heart of every community – the family.*

*Questions for Mother's Day: Given how much they have sacrificed for the sake of their country, for the future of the human race, isn't it time that we accorded these brave young women the recognition, pay and benefits we have always accorded to soldiers? Isn't it time there were statues to The Unknown Mother?*

*(Symbolism used: A red carnation signifies respect of a living mother; white honours a mother who has died.)*

## SOME THOUGHTS FOR EVERY DAY NOT MOTHER'S DAY:

"If men could give birth, then birth would now be an even more prestigious affair than it was in the ancient matriarchies, attended by the same cultural huzzahs that now accompany reaching the top of a mountain, crossing the North Pole or wiping out an enemy machine gun nest."
~ *Barbara G. Walker*

"If men could get pregnant, abortion would be a sacrament."
~ *Florynce Kennedy*

If men *got pregnant, if they* experienced labour, *you know* that abortion would be legal, pregnancy would require generous leave time, birth would command significant health benefits, child-care would be a highly paid profession and war would be unknown.

But it's women who experience it ... and patriarchy decided millennia ago that any activity exclusively female ain't worth spit.


**NOTES**: *Patriarchy = Double Standards.*

*If an activity is male, then it is significant, important, respected (even worshipped) and generally well paid. If an activity is female, then it is insignificant, unimportant, disrespected (even despised) and generally poorly paid or expected to be done for free – woman's work.*

*According to patriarchy, females don't risk life and health, or sell their future when they get pregnant. "No Dear, you're merely 'popping one out of the oven.'"*

Do nothing?

Today, I got you your breakfast, made you lunch, cared for the kids, cleaned the house, did the laundry, dishes and shopping, made everyone's supper and I still have to put the kids to bed and get ready for tomorrow ... all while toting an extra 25 lbs.

In addition to all that, I created a body, a mind, a soul. I pulled the stuff of the Universe into my womb and wove it into a living being. I worked as the righthand of the Goddess, as the Creator of life, as the Divinity of Genesis.

That's one helluva lot of nothing women are expected to do ...

No wonder I am exhausted.

Now, STFU.

---

***NOTES***: *The patriarchy has conditioned men to think the idiotic statement,* **"I'm just a housewife, I don't work,"** *is true ... that women actually sit at home all day doing nothing!*

*It is past time to disabuse society, and men, of this truly stupid, demeaning and fraudulent belief. Women do some of the hardest work in the world, from toting pails of water and collecting firewood, to keeping home, body and soul together, to carrying life and raising the next generation.*

*The corrected statement should be,* **"I'm just a housewife; I do unpaid, unrecognized and unappreciated work."**

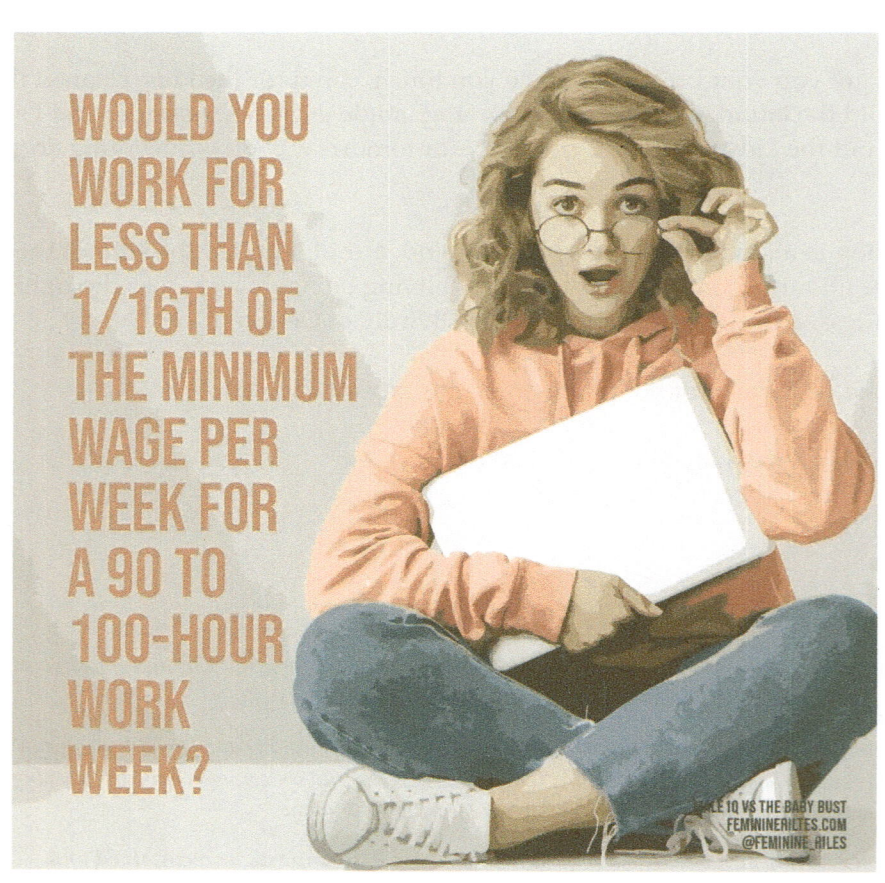

Globally, women are refusing to have children. The result is demographic disaster, a baby bust, with birth rates in over 50% of countries now below the 2.1 needed for a stable population.

Many governments have responded by offering to pay women to stay at home and have babies. *However, the incentives offered are generally worth less than a year's pay at minimum wage.*

Women know that once that bundle of joy arrives, they are facing at least a 16-year commitment. Do the math: That works out to less than $1/16^{th}$ of the annual minimum wage for a 90 to 100-hour work week, with no holidays, benefits or pension.

This tells you everything you need to know about how the patriarchy views female intelligence.

All over the world, women are failing to leap upon these offers causing the men who created them to scratch their heads in puzzlement and ask why their policies aren't increasing fertility rates.

And this tells you everything you need to know about what the patriarchy has done to male intelligence.

GDP not only fails to measure the value of mothers - it also fails to measure the value of Mother Earth.

GDP is never reduced by the depletion of finite resources or by the degradation of our environment.

GDP is always increased by the damage we do to our planet, by species destruction, by ecological disaster, by increasing levels of pollution, and by environmental diseases which destroy our health and our children's future.

GDP is then further increased if we attempt to clean up our mess.

Look on Man's mighty works and despair ...

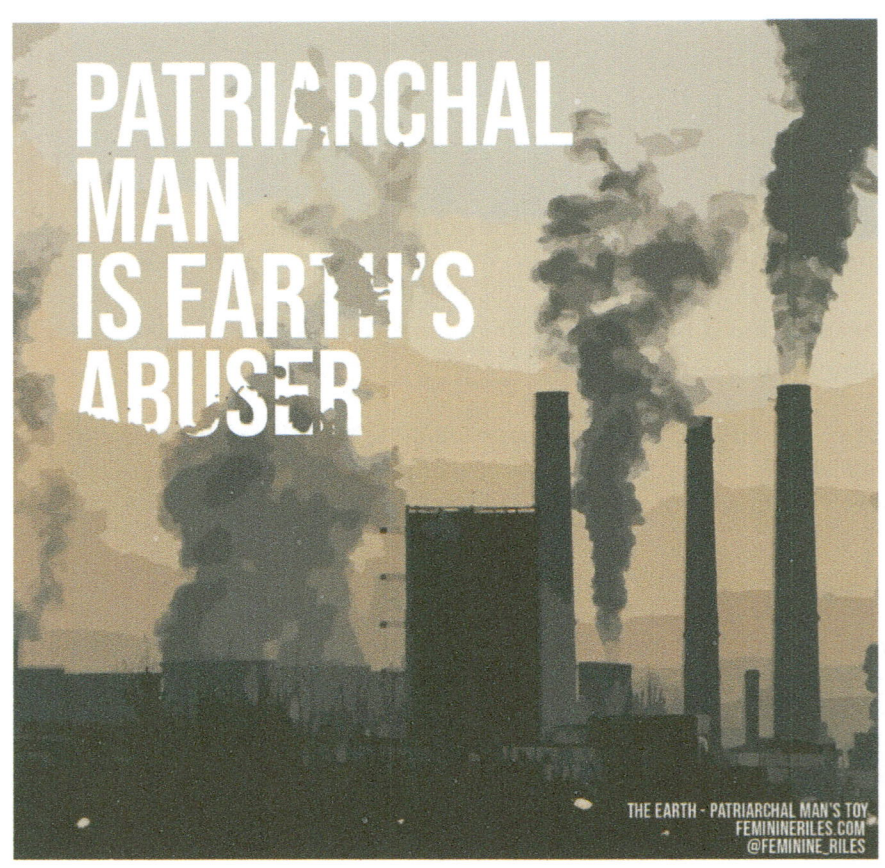

The Earth has been dying since patriarchal man became its master.

The patriarchy is a male dominated society which objectifies the "other" – women, BIPOC, minorities, animals, plants, resources, the environment, our Mother the Earth.

An object is a possession – a toy you are free to use, abuse or destroy as you please. And if the toy gets broken, *why don't you just get a new one*!

The patriarchy produces grown men who are narcissistic egomaniacs, raised as irresponsible, spoiled 3-year-olds: A child who drops his used underwear on the ground, leaves his dirty dishes for others to wash, carelessly walks over a spotless floor with his muddy shoes.

There has *always* been someone there to clean up the patriarchal man's messes for him, to assure him it's not his fault, to get him a new toy – everything has *always* been someone else's problem.

So, patriarchal man is comfortable making a mess of the environment – *someone else's problem*. And if the Earth is destroyed, he believes, just as in the past, and as with all his other toys, *someone will get him a new planet to play with*.

Allowing patriarchal man dominion over the Earth is like giving a wife abuser dominion over a battered woman's shelter.

Sleep with the enemy?

Alas, we women do so much more than that …

We aid and abet them.

We comfort, feed and encourage them.

We assist them to keep us in line and have acquiesced to the myth of the "mighty male" in the rape of our daughters, our land, and our Mother Earth.

The world suffers for our Stockholm Syndrome.

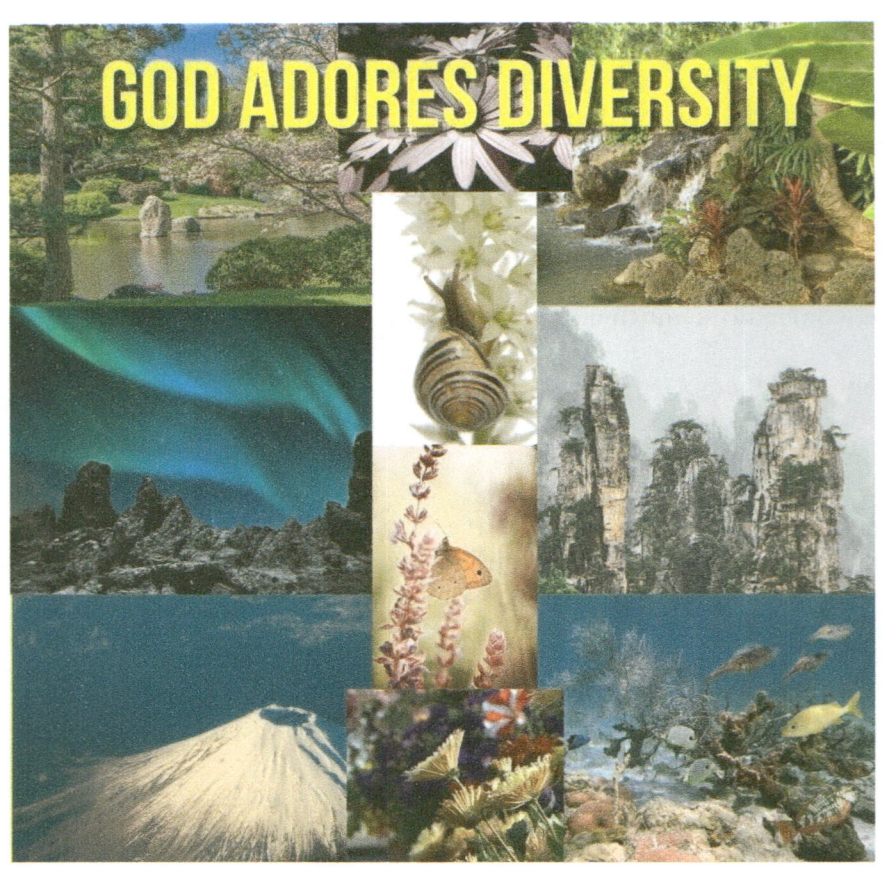

God loves variety.

To look at our world is to see a God who adores diversity, blessing a multitude of features and behaviours:

- 7+ million shades of colour – not one.
- More than 300,000 plant species – not one.
- Nearly a million insect species – not one.
- Over 5,000 kinds of mammals – not one.
- In people, we have straight, bi, gay and trans; short and tall; skinny and fat; white, yellow, black, brown and red; different hair, eyes, IQ, EQ, etc.

Variety is the loving expression of _God_.

But the religious, fundamentalist _man_ loves uniformity.

So, when God's self-appointed male reporter gets around to describing God's desires, somehow God _always_ rejects the vast majority of creation, while preferring a minority.

A minority which – what a miracle! – somehow _always_ just happens to be in the same group our boy belongs to or approves of.

/continued …

***NOTES**: THE CREATOR, whether defined as God or Nature, adores DIVERSITY.*

*Nowhere can you find only "one" of anything. Instead, the universe is an explosion of variety, multiplicity and variability – a rainbow of existences, even within a single species, be they viruses, dogs or humans.*

*It is the religious, fundamentalist, and usually patriarchal MAN who worships UNIFORMITY.*

*His tiny mind reacts with horror to all that The Creator has blessed the world with; he rejects the majority of it, choosing to define "difference" as sinful. He then has the audacity to tell the world **he knows God's will and what God disapproves of** – in other words, if he dislikes something, if he disapproves of it, if he is uncomfortable with it, then God **must feel the same way.***

*And if he can, he will then wipe out that which God created, but which he has arbitrarily decided to be contrary to his **personal** reading of Divine Will.*

*Time to out this narrow belief for the blasphemy it is – no mere man ever gets to dictate to The Creator the acceptable characteristics for life. No mere man gets to say that he, or some other man who preceded him, gets to speak for God, to tell the world what God intended, dumping on God's shoulders responsibility for giving him and his buddies permission for the hatred they spew, the intimidation, harassment and killing they engage in.*

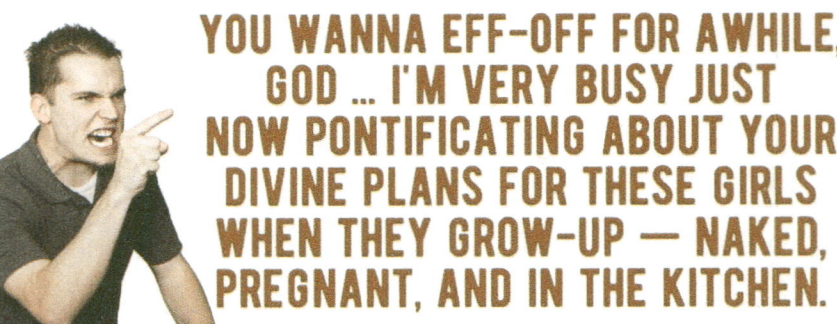

Suppose God blesses a girl with a mind capable of doing math, science, engineering or art; of being an entrepreneur, soldier, sailor or explorer?

What egocentric narcissist dares to question God's wisdom in endowing her with such skills?

What mere man has the audacity to state *it is God's will* that he, or the group he belongs to, gets to forbid her the right to use what God has gifted her with?

**NOTES**: *THE CREATOR, whether defined as God or Nature, has blessed females with brains, ability, imagination, knowledge, wisdom and courage. We have within us the potential to be anything we can dream of ... and so much more.*

*It is the religious, fundamentalist, and usually patriarchal MAN who claims the right to limit, to control, to destroy that which we have been endowed with.*

*His tiny mind reacts with horror to all that The Creator has granted to the female sex; he rejects our humanity, choosing to define us as inferior and incapable.*

/continued ...

*He then has the audacity to tell the world he knows God's will when it comes to what we may do with the sacred gifts we were born with. And if he can, he will confine us to "Kinder, Küche, Kirche", smothering that which God created, but which he has arbitrarily decided to be contrary to his **personal** reading of Divine Will.*

*Time to out this constricting belief for the blasphemy it is – no mere man ever gets to dictate what any person may do with the blessings The Creator has endowed them with.*

*No mere man gets to say that he, or some other man who preceded him, gets to speak for God, to tell the world what God intended, dumping on God responsibility for giving him and his buddies permission to control the life, the dreams, and the hopes of another human being.*

# WHO'S THE WEAKER VESSEL?

THE WEAKER VESSEL
FEMININERILES.COM
@FEMININE_RILES

Man pontificates: "God created women as the weaker vessel, inferior to men."

But history shows that God made women capable of doing (just as well) anything men can do from soldiering to research, from exploration to poetry, from medicine to the arts.

Why would God bless a creature intended to be inferior with such superior abilities?

Man replies not that he was wrong, but that, *"The ways of God are a mystery."*

My mind, talents, body and soul are my own, to make of as I will.

They are gifts from my Creator, to be used and presented back at life's end to that Creator.

What mere man dares to usurp the hand of God and say what I may create of my life? What I may accomplish? What I must or must not do?

Who dares to deprive the artisan of the tools that her Creator gave her?

**NOTES**: *No mere man has the right to dictate to me what I may do with the gifts my Creator endowed me with.*

*What I choose to do with my life is entirely between me and my God – I don't care what you think, I don't care what you believe, I am not interested in your opinion – it is none of your business.*

Considering all of the hypocrisy, atrocities, war and violence committed in His name by those claiming to be His servants ...

Considering how often and badly He has been misrepresented by those claiming to be His servants ...

God must often be heard to mutter, "Geez, it's so hard to get good help."

*NOTES: Patriarchal men have a mental problem. They natter endlessly about love, peace, kindness and charity. But they consistently follow the opposite path.*

*And we wonder why the world is so f\*ked-up?*

Picture credit: Tim Green from Bradford, CC BY 2.0 (https://creativecommons.org/licenses/by/2.0), via Wikimedia Commons https://commons.wikimedia.org/wiki/File:Facepalm_%287839341408%29.jpg)

*Psychology Today* reported on a study in which pairs of participants were asked to complete a task which had been designed to fail.

Most people tended to protect their partner, sharing the blame.

By contrast, narcissists swore it was entirely the other person's fault, eagerly fingering their companion.

And God said to Adam, "Have you eaten from the tree that I commanded you not to eat from?"

And Adam said, "The woman you put here with me – she gave me some fruit from the tree and I ate it." (Genesis 3: 11-12)

Adam the first narcissist?


**NOTES**: *The patriarchy has long used the Adam and Eve story to justify damning females as inferior. Maybe it's time to rethink that story and what it actually tells us about the patriarchy, religion and male prejudices.*

By Domenichino, The Rebuke of Adam and Eve, 1626 - This file was donated to Wikimedia Commons as part of a project by the National Gallery of Art. Please see the Gallery's Open Access Policy., CC0, https://commons.wikimedia.org/w/index.php?curid=74897067

Occasionally a boy is born with female genitalia.

Imagine if Shakespeare, Mozart or Galileo had been born with a vagina instead of a penis. Trapped in a female body, what opportunity would have been given to their genius?

Absolutely none!

As females, their genius would have been ignored, belittled and suppressed.

They'd have been denied an education and the right to use their abilities.

They'd have been taught to keep house and been told that anything else was both beyond and forbidden to them.

**NOTES**: *Beware the Lady-Parts Handicap, my son!*

Biology is NOT destiny.

The fact that a woman is biologically determined to have a womb tells you she MAY GET pregnant.

It tells you nothing whatsoever about what she can or cannot do.

Dogs are genetically programmed as predators – we do not tolerate them hunting our offspring.

Gorilla and chimp vocal cords are genetically designed so that they cannot voice words, yet they have learned to communicate with us using sign language.

"Biological possibility and desire are not the same as biological need. Women have childbearing equipment. For them to choose not to use the equipment is no more blocking what is instinctive than it is for a man who, muscles or no, chooses not to be a weightlifter."
~ *Betty Rollin*


**NOTES**: *Betty Rollin is one of a multitude of talented women who have changed our world ... you, know,* **history** *... but been ignored by* **his-story.**

*She has written books on coping with cancer and death, as well as been the subject of two popular movies.*

*Check her out on Wikipedia.*

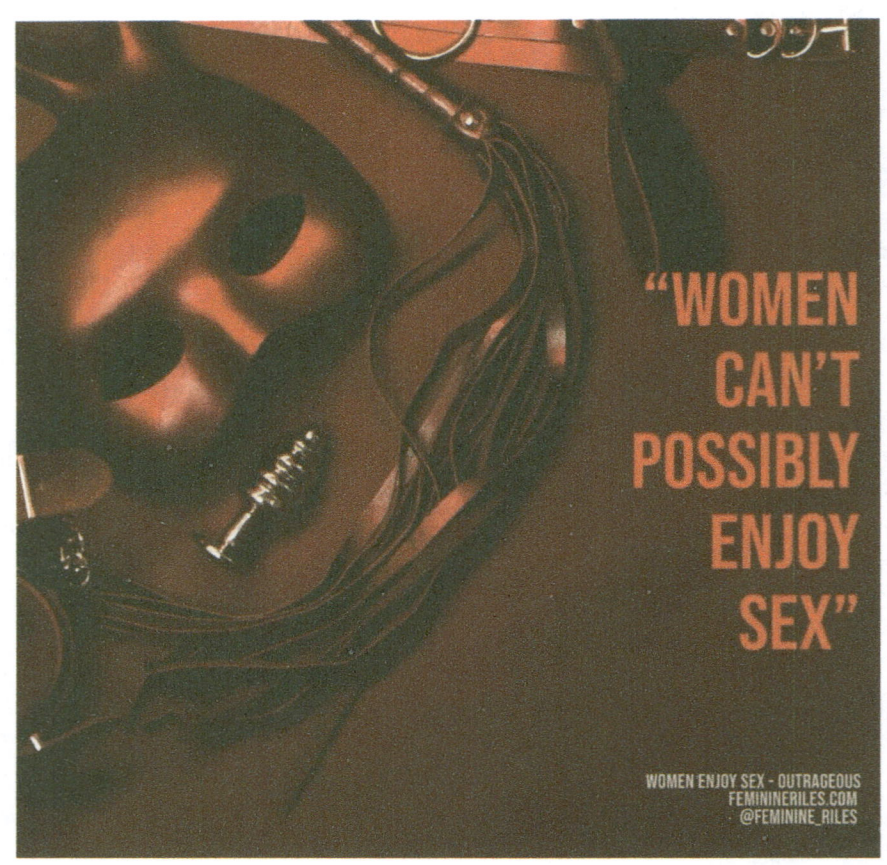

The tiny female clitoris has *over* 8,000 nerve endings – *more than* the entire male penis.

The *only* reason the clitoris exists is to provide women with pleasure.

If men had such a remarkable organ, devoted *only* to providing them with pleasure, well, you know, we'd never hear the end of it.

Science texts would extol its existence and show how it proves male biological superiority, leading naturally to male dominance and female submissiveness.

No wonder they cut it off in so many patriarchal cultures.

And if a patriarchy doesn't *excise* it, they *erase* it – both sexes are kept ignorant of its existence.

*NOTES*: *Women enjoy sex? Outrageous!!! (So saith the patriarchy.)*

Patriarchal men NEVER hesitate to blame some woman for their bad behaviour: What, me? Responsible for my thoughts? For my mouth? For my hands?

It started with Adam and Eve and that all too familiar male refrain ... "Ohhhh, boohoohoo, it's all her fault! She made me do it!" ...

And millennia later, they're STILL blaming the women in their lives for their bad behaviour.

### *Adam's Rib Defense*
Holding women responsible for male weaknesses, their failings, their stupidity.

***NOTES**: When a child gets caught in a bad act, their first defense is often to point at someone else and scream, "They made me do it!"*

*We don't accept this excuse from children.*

*Yet patriarchal laws allow grown men to behave like children. It allows them to point to the victim of their aggression and state, "They made me do it."*

*It then excuses their behaviour as justified.*

*It is well past time to topple this moronic system of oppression, injustice and abuse.*

Men have pontificated for millennia about what women can do, what they can't do, what they ought to do, what they should do, what they must do, what they must not do.

Who do they think they are?

God?

**NOTES**: *The patriarchy accords a man godlike control over women **merely because** he has a prick and she doesn't.*

*A man does not have to have intelligence, integrity or ability. He does not have to be sane, kind, thoughtful or decent. He does not have to be sober or of good character. He does not have to earn respect or prove that he has anything of value to say.*

*It is sufficient for him to point to the bulge in his pants for women to be expected to shut up and obey, without question.*

The patriarchy enforces a simple set of rules:

- Male pursuits are superior.
- Female ones are inferior.

This reflects an ancient logic still deeply embedded in all our psyches:

- Things men do, *no matter how stupid*, are by definition, smart.
- Things women do, *no matter how smart*, are by definition, stupid.

No matter how trivial (sports), how meaningless (pornography), or harmful (killing and maiming, whether in reality or virtually), if it is "male", then it is important, sacred, relevant, prized, recorded, reported-on and highly paid.

No matter how important (bearing the next generation), or meaningful (educating the young), or beneficial (caring for children, the old, the sick), if it is "female", then it is demeaned, trivialized, irrelevant, despised, ignored and poorly paid.

Pornography, sports, war, violence towards others, their degradation, persecution or destruction are the stuff of male superiority.

Love, domestic concerns, harmony, peace, caring for others, their health, happiness and welfare are the stuff of female inferiority.

No wonder the world is so screwed-up and screwed-over.


**NOTES**: *And we ask why the world is so f*ked-up?*

*Thank the patriarchy!*

MY FELLOW PATRIARCHS! THINK OF THE WONDERFUL JOB WE MEN HAVE DONE OF RULING THE WORLD: JUST, HUMANE, REASONABLE, REASONED AND PROFITABLE WAR, GENOCIDE, INEQUALITY, BRUTALITY, SLAVERY OPPRESSION, AND ENVIRONMENTAL DESTRUCTION. **NOW JUST IMAGINE PUTTING WOMEN IN CHARGE!** THINK OF THE HYSTERICAL, CRAZY CONSEQUENCES: WORLD PEACE, EQUALITY, ELIMINATION OF HUNGER AND POVERTY, ALL CHILDREN LOVED AND CARED FOR, OUR ENVIRONMENT RESPECTED, PROFITS IGNORED IN THE NAME OF HUMANITY. IT'S JUST FAR TOO TERRIFYING TO EVEN CONTEMPLATE!

Brain imaging studies show that as men and women watched someone they liked in pain, the empathy centres of their brains were activated.

When it was someone they disliked, women's responses were unchanged.

However, for men, the reward areas in the brain were activated – men take pleasure in the misfortune of a perceived "enemy".

This is why we would *never* want women in charge ... God forbid, peace and genuine love for one's neighbour might break out.


*NOTES: What more need be said?*

# AND NOW, THE GOOD WORD FROM THE PATRIARCHAL HANDBOOK!

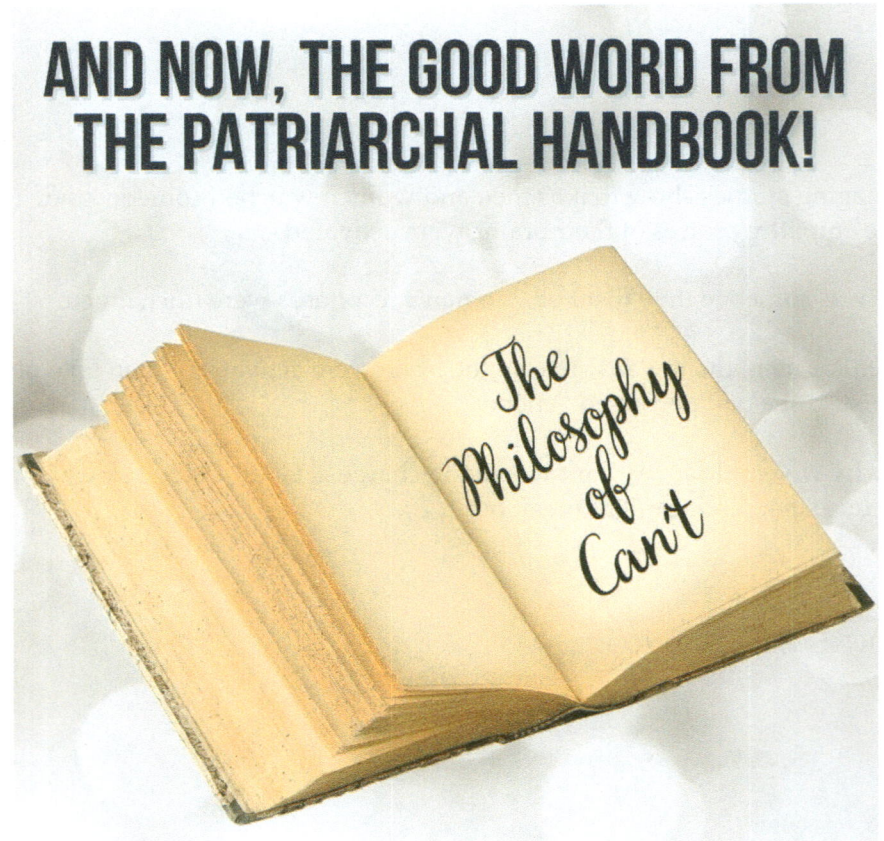

*How The Male Philosophy of Can't Works:*

1. Declare women doing activity X to be taboo or a violation of the laws of God. (Women *can't* do X.)
2. Forbid women to do X. (Women *can't* do X.)
3. Exclude women from education, training, opportunities or options with respect to X. (Women *can't* do X.)
4. Because they are disabled from doing X, women become incapable of doing X. (Women *can't* do X.)
5. Philosophize about how women can't do X because women are inferior. (Hmmmmmph, *stupid* women *can't* do X.)

Men!

The Great Rational-lies-ers.


**NOTES**: *Patriarchy = Inequity*

*In patriarchy, the dominant KNOW they must keep subordinates uneducated, else risk competition which would reveal they aren't as superior as they claim and that subordinates are actually not inferior at all.*

*Inequity is the foundation of patriarchy – and keeping those deemed inferior – women, minorities, anyone not of our race, creed, colour, tribe, beliefs – uneducated is the key to keeping them in submission and subjugation.*

*Isn't it time to topple this dysfunctional system of oppression?*

## *Understanding Male Logik*

Create an unlevel playing field:

- Prevent women from doing X.
- Punish women physically, mentally, emotionally and spiritually if they ever try to do X.

When a few brave women actually do X, pontificate loudly on how it is a flaw in women which prevents the majority of them from doing X.

If Women are the fair sex, then Men are the unfair sex.


**NOTES**: *Patriarchy = Inequity*

*No gurls allowed! This has been patriarchy's mantra for millennia – forbidding women from literacy, education, research, employment, opportunity, even leaving their house.*

*Then "brilliant" male after male piled on to the sisters they had crippled, using their supposedly majestic intellects to prove that women were to blame for failing to "equal" the abilities of men.*

*Philosophers, scientists, mathematicians ... wilfully blind, stupid, bigoted, small-minded rational-lies-ers who have contributed so much to the inequality and misery that is patriarchy.*

*Isn't it time to topple this dysfunctional system of oppression?*

Picture credit: Metropolitan Museum of Art, CC0, via Wikimedia Commons (https://commons.wikimedia.org/wiki/File:A_Militia_Meeting_MET_DP879716.jpg)

# WHY WAS SHE PRONE TO FAINTING?
## CHECK ALL WHICH APPLY:

- ☐ SHE IS WEARING NEARLY 15 POUNDS OF CLOTHES AND UNDERGARMENTS.
- ☐ HER CORSET IS SO TIGHTLY LACED AS TO CUT-OFF BLOOD FLOW AND BREATHING.
- ☐ TO FIT THE CORSET, SHE EATS AND DRINKS INADEQUATE AMOUNTS.
- ☐ HER SHOES ARE TOO SMALL, CAUSING PAIN WITH EVERY STEP.
- ☐ SHE HAS NEVER BEEN ALLOWED TO EXERCISE AND BUILD HER LUNGS, HEART OR MUSCULOSKELETAL SYSTEM.
- ☐ HER COMMUNITY CONSIDERS FAINTING TO BE A DESIRABLE FEMININE TRAIT.
- ☐ IT'S HOT WITH 90% HUMIDITY.
- ☑ SHE IS JUST A **NATURALLY** WEAK AND INFERIOR CREATURE.

Victorian men painted "their" women as inferiors: delicate, feeble, febrile and faint.

Imagine being dehydrated, suffering from malnutrition, never having been allowed to exercise, and living in a society where being weak, pale, wan and subject to fainting is sexually attractive.

Imagine wearing hoop skirts, multiple layers of undergarments and corsets so tightly laced as to cut off blood flow and breathing.

Now imagine all of that on a hot day.


**NOTES**: *Patriarchy = Wilful male blindness and stupidity **proudly** displayed as logic, rational thinking and genius analysis.*

*Patriarchal men love to mock women as their physical inferiors – calling them delicate, fragile and weak.*

*But they **never** consider the handicaps they place on their women before "competing" with them.*

/continued

*Let's see how a man dressed in 15 to 25 pounds of clothing, his torso laced into a corset which cuts off his blood flow and breathing, his health weakened by lack of exercise, dehydration and malnutrition, his feet compressed into shoes too small, his every step restricted by what he wears, functions.*

***Even an idiot should be able to predict the answer – poorly.***

*Yet these men, who claim "superior intellectual abilities", seem unable to figure it out – ascribing weakness in females to their genes instead of to the <u>man</u>-made impairments imposed on them.*

*[Online research showed that the typical Victorian woman's summer outfit weighed approximately 15 pounds; her winter one might weigh as much as 35 pounds. The multiple layers of undergarments, corset, hooped skirt, billowy sleeves, etc. (as in the film, Gone with the Wind) were very heavy, weighing 20 - 25 pounds and incorporating nearly 30 yards of fabric. Beaded ballgowns could weigh in at 75 pounds. A lady of quality would wear up to 10 petticoats as underskirts, covered by a crinoline, a cage-like frame to create a circular shape, and then the dress itself.*

*With so many petticoats, a woman often passed out from overheating. And when she moved, the quantity and weight of material ensured she could take only small steps.]*

*Question:*

What does a patriarchal man do when he cannot understand a woman?

*Answer:*

Always blame it on <u>her</u> hormones.

Never blame it on <u>his</u> ignorance or stupidity.

*NOTES: Patriarchal men are trained to pay little or no attention to females, to what they say, want or need.*

*When this lack of communications leads to misunderstandings, it is just so much easier (and so much more satisfying) to blame her for his failure to engage in any kind of meaningful interaction than to actually change his behaviour.*

*Patriarchal Men*

Creatures who rarely bother to listen to anything of what a woman has said.

They then rush to express their opinion:

"Who can understand women?"


*NOTES: Patriarchal men are taught to ignore what females say they feel, want or need.*

*When this inevitably leads to confusion, it is just so much easier (and satisfying) to fall back on that old chestnut, "Who can understand women?" than to actually change male beliefs.*

Think of the endless barriers to talent and ability that the dominant male has put in front of race, sex and disability.

Whenever minorities, women and the handicapped have spoken, asked for respect, begged for equal opportunity, it has been close to impossible to get heard.

They have almost always been forced to resort to exaggerated or bad behaviour to get recognition for what is inside rather than for what is outside.

***NOTES**: Stay silent and get passed over, underpaid, used and abused.*

*Speak up and be accused of being pushy, obnoxious, demanding, not a team-player and difficult.*

*Damned if you do; damned if you don't.*

Dominant males prefer to keep women and minorities where they belong.

Out of *their* schools, *their* jobs, *their* clubs and *their* entitlements.

75 years ago, Tiger Woods would not have entered the exclusive links he now plays on unless he'd been a caddy, waiter, janitor or security guard. He is where he is because Blacks fought, they marched, they threatened, they sued.

From the perspective of polite society, they were loud, mouthy, obnoxious, pushy, demanding, dangerous and criminal.

But today, If Tiger Woods were to say, "Who me, a desegregationist?", polite society would see him as an ungrateful bastard.

Yet, these days, a woman is too often considered by polite society an ungrateful bastard if she does *not* denounce feminism and revile her liberators.

***Sisters! You don't change the world by following the rules; by being a "good girl", polite and well-behaved.***

You most assuredly do not change the world by:

- Being embarrassed by the "bad" behaviour of those who forced open the doors you now waltz through.
- Disparaging the sacrifices they made to give you choices they were denied.
- Refusing to follow in their brave footsteps and holding those doors open for the women and minorities who want to follow you.

In my grandmother's time, a respectable woman's sole career path was daughter, wife, mother.

She suffered from a congenital crime: Being born female.

Her penance: She was expected to devote herself to a life of unpaid service.

Her crowning achievement: To produce a son.

It ought to terrify any modern, educated and liberated young Ms. who claims **not to be a feminist** to realize that if women like my grandmother had conformed, chosen to belong to a "nice" society, to be seen as normal, to be praised as "feminine", then that was the limit of her identity *and* it would now be the limit of yours.

*NOTES: Are you as tired as I am of females who get to enjoy the outcomes of feminism, taking for granted its hard-won successes, while bad-mouthing the memory of those who fought so hard for our collective future?*

In my grandmother's time, at the dawn of the 20th century, a woman was not a person. She could not vote; if she attended university, many of them refused to bestow a degree on a female, regardless of her marks.

She was treated like a child. She could not own a bank account; nor could she borrow money in her own name. Most jobs were forbidden to her, but if she did land a job, she got paid less than the lowest male employee, and by law, she could not belong to any firm's pension fund.

Once she married, everything she owned (money, land, investments, a house, etc.) AUTOMATICALLY TRANSFERRED into her husband's name. After marriage, she could no longer hold property or earn an income in her own name.

Her children also belonged to her husband, meaning they could be stripped from her at divorce.

She could be committed to a mental institution for life by her husband, with NO QUESTIONS ASKED, and drugged or lobotomized into a zombie. She could be tossed from the family home with only the clothes on her back (with hubby keeping the property she brought into the marriage with her).

*/continued*

In my grandmother's grandmother's time, women were chattels, with no voice and no rights - merely property, which, along with her children, could be sold to any passing stranger, as described in a famous episode from Thomas Hardy's novel, *The Mayor of Casterbridge*.

How about some gratitude?

Think about all of that, and instead of carping about feminism, say a fervent *"Thank you"* to every woman who opened doors FOR YOU; to every feminist who fought FOR YOUR RIGHTS ...

Hail to every person who has ever been in the battle for human rights, for equality, for a better world and a brighter future. THANK YOU, FEMINISM! because of you, we have made huge steps forward.

Now we have to keep marching forward to even greater change, to a world of equality for all ... CHARGE!!!

***NOTES***: *Women who enjoy education, a job, freedom to travel, who own property or a bank account, who invest or borrow (e.g., have a credit card), who are blessed with rights our foremothers lacked, are ungrateful traitors to deny feminism, which fought to win them those rights.*

A common misperception is that gender equality benefits women at the expense of men. In fact, it is *not* a zero-sum game - female wins are *not* male losses.

**Instead, Feminism makes men much better-off on all dimensions.**

Studies using global dbases reveal that in more gender equal countries:

- Males experience greater happiness and much higher quality of life. They sleep better, live longer, have better mental and physical health and a lower likelihood of suffering from a divorce, domestic violence, depression, suicide or a violent death.

- Men score higher on economic well-being due to stronger economies, greater prosperity, reduced poverty and increased spending on social services, education, healthcare and development.

- A male is freed from toxic norms and stereotypes. He is empowered to be who he is, to show a wider range of emotions, to bond with his family, and to choose a career which expresses himself, since jobs are less likely to be sex-typed.

/continued

- Adolescent boys have fewer psychosomatic complaints, are less anti-social, and are more likely to use contraceptives. Male survivors of violence have a voice, leading to a reduction in the incidence of such assaults.

- Men have better relationships with their children due to improved family leave and acceptance of them playing a greater role in parenting. Their children are happier and healthier; they do better in school and are less likely to need psychiatric care/medication. Child abuse is reduced by almost two-thirds.

- Men experience more sex, greater sexual satisfaction, better and more stable relationships with women, increased marital happiness, and reduced family friction.

Feminism has transformed the lives of all - women and men, girls and boys - for the better. Feminism benefits males by improving their happiness, health, wealth, relationships, welfare, sexual satisfaction and well-being.

Feminism says: You're welcome, Guys!

*NOTES: Feminism benefits males by improving their happiness, health, wealth, relationships, welfare, sexual satisfaction and well-being.*

*What's not to like, guys?*

*9 things women couldn't do in 1971*
*(or why we need feminism)*

1. Open a bank account, have a credit card, or apply for a loan without your husband's permission.
2. Keep your job after you became pregnant.
3. Serve on a jury.
4. Serve in military combat (but you could die, be raped or maimed in war).
5. Get an Ivy League education: Elite colleges did not accept females (e.g., Harvard did not accept women until 1977; Columbia until 1983).
6. Sue for workplace harassment.
7. Refuse your husband permission to have sex with you.
8. Pay the same as men for health insurance - you paid more even though females are better health risks than males.
9. Get contraceptives without your husband's permission.

*/continued*

RBG: BELOVED WIFE, HAPPILY MARRIED TO MARTIN GINSBURG FOR 56 YEARS (SEE HIS ADORATION AS HE LOOKS AT HER). MOTHER AND GRANDMOTHER.

SHE WANTED A BETTER WORLD FOR HER CHILDREN AND GRANDCHILDREN AND FOUGHT TIRELESSLY TO WIN IT FOR THEM AND FOR ALL OF US.

*NOTES:*

*Ruth Bader Ginsburg changed the American legal landscape: She fought countless discrimination cases, arguing 6 gender inequity cases before an all-male supreme court, winning 5.*

*She blessed women with a better life.*

*MUCH NEEDED and IMPORTANT REMINDER: Women must learn about what their foremothers did for them and instead of turning against them, calling them ugly man-haters, be honouring and thanking them. We need to understand just how recently, and how hard won, so much of the progress we take for granted occurred. Any woman 55 years, or older, lived through these times.*

*Never forget how many people would love to return us to these times. Rights, as Gilead and Texas demonstrate, can be stripped from you in an instant. And, finally, remember that millions of women globally still live under these restrictions and far worse.*

*"Feminism is NOT just for other women. KNOW your HERstory."*
*~ Old Crone (Based on Twitter post by Old Crone: https://twitter.com/wpcelebration/status/1165802724736155648?lang=en)*

*Verified by Snopes.*

*Chrysanthemums honour the dead, with white ones for the departed souls of mothers.*

Photos: SCOTUS Photographer: Steve Petteway [1] - SCOTUS (Source 2), Public Domain, https://commons.wikimedia.org/w/index.php?curid=55329542 / Pete Souza - P081209PS-0299, Public Domain, https://commons.wikimedia.org/w/index.php?curid=79243318

My Dear Husband:
I know you deserted me and the boys a decade ago, moving to a different country, but the bank says I need your permission for a mortgage.

So, I am writing to beg your assistance with this matter.

A mere 50 years ago, my aunt, a successful entrepreneur, needed her deadbeat husband's permission for a mortgage to buy a house for herself and her two sons.

She told the bank he had deserted her and had moved to another country.

She was ordered to write to him.

A useless man in the bush was worth more than a successful woman in the hand.

**NOTES**: *Anyone who thinks feminism has not improved the lives of women should hear some of the stories of my feisty female ancestors! They went on to found businesses, get degrees, become professionals, change the world for the better, as well as fall in love with men, marry, and have families.*

*And every step of the way,* **merely because they were female**, *they had to constantly battle patriarchal beliefs and restrictions.*

*Feminism has bravely fought to give today's Woman rights and freedoms that my ancestors could only dream of. But the war is not yet won, despite the many successful battles, patriarchy is still in charge.*

*Past time to put an end to this repressive regime!*

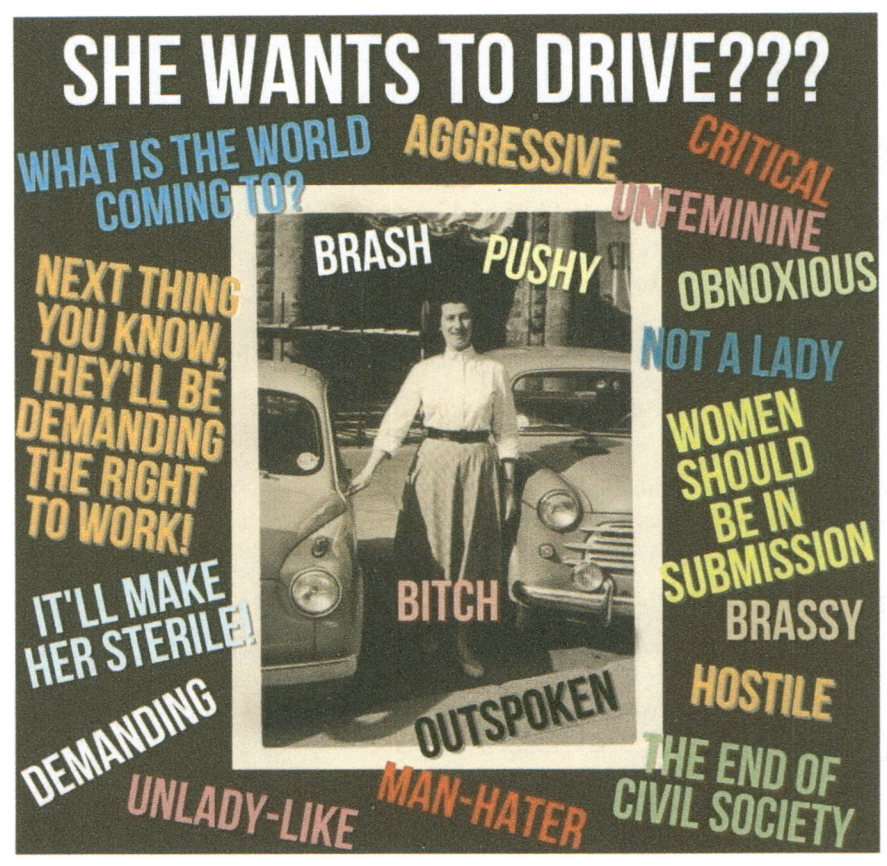

For millennia, men were in the driver's seat. Women were taught they had no options, other than being a wife and a mother, and no right to an opinion on anything, including their own lives and futures. Men decided everything for them.

300 years of women who were brassy, obnoxious, outspoken, critical, hostile, "unfeminine" and demanding fighters bought you control over your life and your rights and freedoms.

Look around you at how the majority of the world's women live today … the lessons are simple: Be a feminist; guard what was so hard-earned. Never forget what was bought with blood can be lost in an instant if we drop our guard.

*NOTES: According to family tradition, some of the things my grandmother heard when she asked for driving lessons.*

*She never did learn to drive and all her life was dependent on others to get around.*

Most oppressed peoples honour the memory of those who fought for their rights; they are proud of those who sought to give them freedom.

So, why do so many women get uncomfortable when asked if they are feminists? Why aren't we proud of the gutsy women who fought for our freedom and rights? Why are we embarrassed by the necessary behaviour of those who prised opened doors for us? Why do we apologize for our justified beliefs?

Even worse are the women who insult and degrade our brave foremothers who fought so hard for our rights, calling them ugly man-haters merely because they questioned patriarchal oppression.

They are ungrateful, craven and traitors to their sex - and that is even truer if they are Western women who have benefited from an education, able to pursue a decent job and an opportunity to become what they dream to be - from housewife to astronaut to political leader to whatever.

Such women should have to trade places with an Afghani girl - someone who would appreciate the gifts that ungrateful Western woman spat upon.

*/continued*

***NOTES***: *I am so sick of hearing the statement, "Who me, a feminist? Not me," from ungrateful women who deny our heroic foremothers, but have had no hesitation accepting the benefits feminism has bestowed upon them.*

*I am even sicker of hearing some idiot female bitching that feminists are ugly man-haters, while enjoying the freedoms that our beautiful and caring foremothers - most of them were married and loved their families - bravely carved for us out of a patriarchy that was once much like Afghanistan when it came to women: No say, no freedom, no education, no opportunity, no rights, and no future other than housewife, maid, nanny or whore.*

*You could be bought and sold like a cow, and ditto for your children. You were not allowed to write, create or invent in your own name. Your property at marriage went to your husband to piss away as he pleased, leaving you and your kids to starve. You could be committed to an institution for life, or your children stripped from you, on just your husband's say-so.*

*No, you can't trade places with my great-grandmother who knew all of those oppressions ... but damn it all, if you don't like what feminism has gifted you with, then give up your spot at the table to an Afghani girl, who would actually appreciate the rights and freedoms you seem so eager to spit upon.*

Western women sit down to the banquet that feminism prepared for them, to a feast of life, to choices that most women in history never tasted and that most women around the world are still denied.

They fill their plates, while they damn the Chef ...

"*I'm* not a feminist!"


*NOTES: Educated? Have a job, freedom to travel, own property/a bank account, able to invest or borrow?*

*Then you have rights our FEMINIST foremothers fought for.*

*If you are going to enjoy their gift, at least have the decency to be grateful to the movement which delivered it.*

*Better yet, stop biting the hand which opened so many opportunities for the women and girls of our generation ... join the cause ... do it for the sake of coming generations ... if you have eyes to see, ears which hear, **you know** there is so much which still needs to be fixed to make this a better world for all.*

Rights take years, sometimes decades, even centuries, to win.

**Rights are bought with blood; it takes only a lapse of attention to lose them.**

"Our lives begin to end the day we become silent about things that matter."
~ *Martin Luther King*

**NOTES**: *If you are familiar with **The Handmaid's Tale**, or have been following the news on what is happening in Texas and other "conservative" US states, as well as in Afghanistan, China, India, etc., then heed this warning …*

Freedom is <u>not</u> free ... it is bought at high cost. It is maintained by constant diligence. If you don't protect your freedom someone will take it away from you.
~ *Florynce Kennedy*

Counter-movements among racists and sexists and nazifiers are just as relentless as dirt on a coffee table ... every housewife knows that if you don't sooner or later dust ... the whole place will be dirty again.
~ *Florynce Kennedy*

Freedom is like taking a bath: You got to keep doing it every day.
~ *Florynce Kennedy*

When a system of oppression has become institutionalized it is unnecessary for individuals to be oppressive.
~ *Florynce Kennedy*

You've got to rattle your cage door. You've got to let them know that you're in there and that you want out. Make noise. Cause trouble. You may not win right away, but you'll sure have a lot more fun.
~ *Florynce Kennedy*

There are very few jobs that actually require a penis or a vagina. All other jobs should be open to everybody.
~ *Florynce Kennedy*

*/continued*

*NOTES: Florynce Rae Kennedy (February 11, 1916 – December 21, 2000), R.I.P.*

*Florynce Kennedy was an African-American lawyer, feminist, civil rights advocate, lecturer and social activist. A warrior for female and black rights, she battled the patriarchy and oppression, fighting institutionalized racism and sexism.*

*Read about her on Wikipedia.*

*Hear her words and pay close attention to her warnings about how freedom and rights can be lost if we fail to defend them.*

> ***Hail to a brave foremother who opened doors, smashed barriers, and left the world a better place.***

Why is it that men who squawk the loudest about their manliness – you know, their bravery, strength, virility and fortitude - are the most interested in marrying a doormat?

Would a tiger be afraid of a tigress?

Do lions prefer to couple with bunny rabbits?

*NOTES: In nature, survival of the fittest is the mantra for both sexes when it comes to producing the next generation. Indeed, for a male, a strong, healthy, intelligent, competent and capable female is the way to ensure that his offspring are both vigorous and have a maximum chance of surviving to reproduce.*

*Patriarchy has turned this natural rule upside down, killing off the strongest of its males in wars, leaving the elderly, decrepit and weak ones to reproduce, while seeing "sexiness" in females who are sickly, frail, helpless and witless.*

*Our species has been around for over 500 millennia. In a mere 3 to 4 of those millennia, the patriarchy has created the perfect recipe for human extinction: Weaken our gene pool, poison our children's food and water, and destroy our Mother the Earth.*

*Time to topple this idiotic and unnatural system of destruction and extinction.*

*Tanya*
Russian peasant, built like an ox, strong enough to pull a plow like a draft horse. In World War II, she joined the Russian army, rising to sergeant. Deadly expert with a knife, a gun, a garrote ... she led men into brutal combat, killing Nazi soldiers with her bare hands.

*Tanya*
One of the most feminine women I ever met. She loved high heels, frilly dresses, polished nails, jewellery, make-up, her hair perfectly coiffed.

Though she could easily have beaten him senseless, she was devoted to her husband, always deferred to his every wish. Demure, obedient, she loved taking care of her home and her family. She was the perfect housewife and a wonderful mother.

*Patriarchy lies.*

A woman can be tough, strong, independent, a fighter, a hero, a leader *and* be feminine, a devoted wife, a wonderful lover and friend, and a great mother.